Reincarnation

DESCRIBED and EXPLAINED

BOOKLET #34

EMMET FOX

DeVorss Publications
Camarillo, California

Reincarnation

ISBN: 978-087516-761-9

DeVorss & Company, Publisher
P.O. Box 1389
Camarillo CA 93011-1389
www.devorss.com

Printed in the United States of America

THE IMPRISONED SPLENDOUR

Truth is within ourselves; it takes no rise
from outward things, what e'er you
may believe.

There is an inmost center in us all,

Where truth abides in fulness; and around,

Wall upon wall, the gross flesh hems it in,

This perfect clear perception—which is
truth.

A baffling and perverting carnal mesh

Binds it, and makes all error; and to know

Rather consists in opening out a way

Whence the imprisoned splendour may
escape,

Than in effecting entry for a light

Supposed to be without.

BROWNING

Reincarnation

HAVE you ever asked yourself why there should be such a difference between one human lot and another? Have you ever wondered why some people seem to be so happy and fortunate in their lives, while others appear to undergo so much undeserved suffering? I am sure you have, because only a very selfish or a very thoughtless person could fail to be challenged sooner or later by this problem.

Why is one person so well placed in life, having apparently everything done for him; being born into a nice family, carefully brought up, given every advantage that money and culture can confer, sent to good schools, and launched into life with every advantage?

Why is another boy or girl born into very difficult circumstances, where it is all but impossible to make any advance in life?

Why is one child born a cripple, or born

blind, or born with some horrible disease; while another child arrives in this world with a strong, clean, healthy little body, certain to grow up well and sturdy?

Why does one child reach manhood or womanhood, and live to a ripe old age, whereas another child is born, and after only a few weeks, or a few months, or even a few years, dies, without seemingly having lived to any purpose? In a certain old country churchyard, there is a tombstone dating from the seventeenth century. It marks the grave of an infant who died after three weeks, and the epitaph reads: *Since so soon done, why was I begun?* And, indeed, the question is an extremely searching one.

Such questions call urgently for an answer if we are to believe in the existence of God, and in a universe governed by law and order. To the honest and fearless soul, the problem of the inequality of human lives is one that clamors for solution.

Men and women are not born free and

equal. They are *created* free and equal, but they are not *born* so. The Declaration of Independence does not say that men are *born* free and equal. It says that they are *created* so, which is quite a different thing. Men and women are not born free and equal but start this life like horses in a handicap race—no two bearing an equal burden. Now, why should this be, if indeed God is Love, and if God is just, and if God is all powerful?

Well, the answer is that this life that you are living today is not the only life; and that it cannot be understood when judged by itself. The answer is that you have lived before, not once, but many, many times, and that in the course of these many lives you have *thought* and *said* and *done* all sorts of things, good and bad, and that the circumstances into which you were born are but the natural outcome of the way in which you have lived and comported yourself in your former lives. You are reaping today, for good or evil, the results of the seeds that you have sown during these many previous lives. The Bible says, "Whatsoever a man soweth, that shall he also reap"; and that text states the truth, and it cannot be made to mean anything else.

You who read these words have lived many, many times before, in different ages, in different conditions, under different skies, and in different civilizations. Many times you have been a man, and many times you have been a woman. You have probably been very rich, and very poor; and probably, you have sometimes been highly placed in the world, and sometimes your place has been lowly. Some of those who are at the bottom of our social ladder today have walked the earth as kings, and presidents, and generals, and admirals, and high priests; and some who now sit in the seats of the mighty, surrounded by pomp and circumstance, have toiled as simple peasants in days gone by, pulled at the oar of a galley, or worn the chains of the slave. And you, yourself, in future ages, centuries from now very likely, will return to this earth planet and be born again as a baby in some family; and grow up, and probably marry, and live out another life. And the conditions under which you start that life, will be the outcome of the lives you have already lived; but most particularly will they be the outcome of the life which you are living at the present time. That, briefly, is the story of the life of man. What is customarily called a lifetime is really but a comparatively brief day in a long, long life.

This is the glorious truth, and it is the most wonderful and beautiful thing that you could ever discover. It is the door of liberation. It is your Charter of Freedom, your passport to Fullness of Life. It means nothing less than that your destiny is in your own hands, and that you may determine that destiny—that you may really make your future life, beginning today, the sort of thing that you wish it to be.

You arrived in this world as a tiny baby, unconscious; and then came consciousness with the first breath; and then your new life had begun. Probably the first thing that happened to you when you came into the world was that they spanked you, and in most cases, until you know the Law and practice it, the world will go on spanking you until the very end—until nature gets tired of you and turns you out. You came into the world with a cry—with the very first breath you drew you gave a cry—and many people spend their whole lives crying and protesting, right down to the grave. When, however, you understand that this present life is only one day in your *long* life, and that at the change called death you simply disappear onto the next plane, to come back again later on, then the events of this particular life appear in their true proportion, *and then you begin to have dominion.* The events of this life will not appear less important because of your new knowledge, but they will no longer intimidate you, because you will know that you can control them. No seeming misfortune will any longer have power to break your heart or weaken your courage. You will understand life as the wondrous opportunity and the glorious gift that it is.

People often say that they are sick of this life anyway, that they do not like the world, and that they do not want to come back; but this attitude usually arises from a misunderstanding. It is not really this earth life that they dislike, but the limited or unsatisfactory conditions in which they are finding themselves at present. They fail to realize that they will not, in any case, come back to anything like their present conditions.

You, personally, will probably come back again; but you are not likely to come back for five hundred years or so anyway, and so, obviously, you will not come back to the world you know today. You will return to a very different world, with different conditions, different ways of life, different institutions, different food, and clothing, and social customs, and, above all, to a world full of new and different problems. Most, if not all, of mankind's present problems will have been worked out in one way or another by that time. Most, if not all, existing institutions will have disappeared. All the things that you dislike or disapprove of in the world today will have gone, but, by the same token, most or all of the things that you particularly like and approve of will have gone too—and so when you do arrive it will be for a completely fresh start. It is true that you will have to meet the same *types* of problems, the fundamental types that arise out of the essential character of human nature; but the *conditions* will be utterly different; and the experiences of this life, and all the things that you learned this time will be with you, and will stand you in good stead.

You will not only come back, but you will probably meet some of your present associates again, particularly if there is an emotional link either of love or hatred between you. Love will take care of itself; but you must get all hatred out of your heart, if you do not want to renew disagreeable contacts.*

In the same way, some of your present associates are sure to be people with whom you had dealings in a previous life or lives. Your son today may have been your father, or merely an acquaintance in days gone by, and a close friend today may in other times have been a relative or a husband, or wife. The general tendency is for people who live and move in the same groups to rein-

*See the *Lord's Prayer*, p. 36.

carnate about the same time, though, of course, there will always be exceptions.

I said that you personally will *probably* come back again, and here the question naturally arises—*is it absolutely necessary to come back?* Must we positively come back whether we wish to or not, or however strongly we may prefer not? And the answer is, no, it is not absolutely necessary to come back, but the only way to avoid doing so is a way that hardly anyone will take. You need not come back if you will concentrate your whole heart upon God, seek His presence until you realize it *vividly*, and live to do His Holy Will, and that alone; first, last, and all the time. If you can really do this, and it is of all tasks the most difficult, then you will leave this earth planet to enter into full communion with God, and you need never come back. You will be, as the Bible says, a pillar in the house of God, and need go out no more. Hardly anyone, however, is really prepared to do this at present, and so we have to go on by stages, gradually getting nearer to God as the ages go by, learning slowly from experience or rapidly through study, prayer, and meditation; living life after life until at last we "grow up" spiritually—when the day breaks and the shadows flee away.

The reason why the Bible nowhere definitely teaches Reincarnation and, in fact, avoids the subject, is because the Bible teaches us to concentrate on the task of achieving our reunion with God instead of postponing this indefinitely as many Eastern people do. The doctrine of Reincarnation when not thoroughly understood sometimes tends to make people apathetic and fatalistic. The Bible encourages men to seek actively to liberate themselves from all limitations.

At the same time, it must be remembered that this earth life can be a most interesting and joyous process in itself, for this is a wonderful world (of which even now man only knows about five per cent) and your sojourn here can be a series of wonderful and joyous adventures, if only you will learn the laws of life and apply them. You are not obliged to be sick, or sad, or lonely, or frustrated, or unsuccessful. This life and the lives that follow it, can be made interesting, and joyous, and free.

When I speak of seeking whole-heartedly for God, and putting Him first, I do not mean that you have to spend all your time in church-going, or even in prayer and meditation. That would be unwise. It would be doing as the Anchorites and Hermits of ancient times did. They went into the desert, or climbed on top of a tall pillar to be alone, to get away from temptation and difficulty—but that is not the way. In most cases they merely spent the time in thinking about themselves all day long, and this naturally brought serious troubles upon them. Progress is made by overcoming the practical difficulties of our everyday lives, not by running away from them. Jesus, knowing this, said that he would not pray that his followers should be taken out of the world, but rather that they should remain in the world and develop naturally there. And, indeed, that is just what the world is for. Practical life is the school for spiritual development and the overcoming of selfishness and fear. Your duty is to fill your place in life, whatever it may be for the time being, to the very best of your ability, and to try sincerely to live up to the highest that you know at the moment.

Of course, a definite time must be set aside daily for prayer and meditation, but the rest of the time must be used for incorporating your spiritual understanding into your practical life; for thus only can you yourself progress and help the world too.* So far from being a recluse or an

*The Fifteen Points Card (No. 29) should be studied on this point.

Anchorite, you can make friends, go about the world, visit the theatre, read the newspapers, travel abroad, join clubs and associations, and do all the customary things that people do, but you must do them in the light of your spiritual understanding. Your understanding must mould your activities and your environment; you must not allow your environment to mould you. You must live, so far as you can, as consciously the expression of God, and as His witness and representative.

Why is Reincarnation necessary? Why should life have to develop in that particular way? The reason is this: We are here on the earth planet to learn certain lessons. We are here to develop spiritually. We are here to acquire full understanding of and control over our mentality; and this cannot be done in one lifetime. Why not? Why do we come back, and back, and back many times to this earth for short excursions of perhaps seventy or eighty years instead of, let us say, finishing it up in one very long lifetime of perhaps a thousand or even several thousand years? The explanation lies in man's mental laziness and inertia; in his reluctance to change himself radically, to pull himself out of a rut when once he gets into it, to adopt new ideas and adapt himself to changing conditions. The explanation lies in man's conservatism and tendency to self-satisfaction and, above all, in his ignorance of his own unlimited potentialities—and these are just the very things that he is here to overcome.

Consider again the life of man as we know it in almost every case. He arrives as a new-born baby with no conscious memory of the past. Even his consciousness of the present is at first very limited. Then gradually that consciousness expands and he begins to know his surroundings, to recognize his mother or his nurse. He smiles at them and understands their smiles and caresses. He begins to learn elementary facts concerning life on this plane. He learns to judge distances by feeling out with his hands, discovering that he can touch the side of the cradle, but not the ceiling. He experiences both hunger and satisfaction, both pain and bodily ease.

Gradually he learns to talk, and with the equipment of even a few words his means of communication and of control over his little life is immensely enhanced. He learns the very difficult business of walking. (You have forgotten about it now, but it was a terrible job at the time, that learning to balance and to walk. You tumbled about and bumped your head and cut your knees for a while, but presently you got tired of that and learned to walk safely.) Presently the baby learns to read and to write. These again are very difficult accomplishments—at the time. (You scribble off a letter now, or you skim through a newspaper at great speed, but there was a time when words like "cat" and "dog" presented a real difficulty either to read or write.)

The child goes on learning. Being young, he is interested in everything and wants to know about everything. He pesters his elders with questions on every conceivable subject. (Parents are never tired of telling about their children's thirst for knowledge. "What do you think Johnny asked his father last night?" mother will say.) So the child has this insatiable curiosity, the ceaseless desire to see everything and go everywhere and handle and experiment with everything. We call it play, or getting into mischief, but it really means tasting and investigating life.

So he grows and expands, goes through school and perhaps college, and then out into the world. Here the same process continues. He seeks new experience, wants to do things in new ways, looks at old things with a fresh mind, *and wants to improve everything*. Of course he gets snubbed and rebuffed a good deal, but at first he does not allow this to daunt him. He is young, in the twenties let us say, and to be young is just this very thing. To be young is to have this interest and joy in living for its own sake, to have this appetite for new ideas and new ways, this freedom from fixed mental habits and emotional commitments. That is youth, and that is the consciousness where the morning stars sing together and the children of God shout for joy.

But presently something happens. The glory that is youth lasts for a time, and then . . . and then . . . well then something else begins to happen. That avid interest in all things, that readiness for the new and the untried, begins—insensibly at first—to fade a little, and discouragements and disappointments of one kind or another gradually begin to tell.

The strong race suggestions all around

him gradually get their way. He begins to acquire vested interests (mentally) in the status quo. He begins to settle down. He drops emotional anchors into the sea of life, and these things lead, psychologically, to a diminution of energy. The idea of letting-well-enough-alone begins to appeal to him—and the malignant disease called middle age has set in.

As a boy of twelve he thought he could do anything he wanted to do, reasonable or unreasonable, from being a lion tamer in the circus or the driver of a fire engine, to President of the country. At twenty he thought he could do anything within reason—and he probably could. He might be a little nervous about it, but in his heart of hearts he really thought that he could do anything that any other fellow could do—and that is youth. When he read or heard of some brilliant achievement, no matter how magnificent, he whispered to himself "Well, I could do that too"—and that is youth. But "shades of the prison house begin to close about the growing boy," and now the time has come when he thinks instead, "How wonderful that is: of course I could never do anything like that: I am not in that class: I haven't the ability, or the training, or the money, or the right contacts," or else, "It is now too late." That is middle age, and it comforts itself with all kinds of promises and deceptions and foolish rationalizations as the wheels of life slow down toward the end.

Now you will see that nature could have no object in keeping this middle-aged man alive for hundreds or thousands of years, because he is no longer of much use to her. Nature wants to do new things in new ways, always something new and something better; and the crystallized mentality is not ready for this. So her only remedy, when crystallization sets in, is to remove him from the earth plane altogether; send him to the etheric planes for rest, reflection, assimilation, and general readjustment; and then bring him back again once more as a baby, to experience a new youth and a new period of true spiritual production.

There are other reasons why the reincarnating of the ego many times is necessary, although they really arise from the fact which we have just been considering. Nature wants you to have all kinds of experience in order to develop every side of your character. You need to have been a man and you need to have been a woman, to have been a parent and also a child. You need to learn lessons of discipline and self-restraint, and you need to learn to use authority in the right way. You need to learn the lesson of getting on with other people, and you must also learn to be alone. You must learn to value health and rational living even if you have to learn it through the discipline of sickness. You must learn to bear failure and disappointment with fortitude and you must learn to stand success without allowing your head to be turned. You have to develop such an understanding faith in the unseen that you can find the things that are seen slipping away from you without panic. You have to learn the lesson of patience, and the lesson of enterprise and adventure too; and, above all, you have to move about in time and space that you may learn that nothing that God made is really strange or foreign or separate—and this could not be done in one incarnation.

This is why Reincarnation is necessary. You will see now what a simple and natural process it is. The idea seems a strange and startling one at first only because we in the West have been totally unaware of it. But in the East it is as familiar a fact as the rising and setting of the sun, and it is probable that the majority of mankind have always believed in Reincarnation.

People who accept this truth sometimes prefer to call it by another name—Reproduction, Counterfesance, or Metempsychosis, or some other title—but the principle is the same; the reappearance on the earth of the same individual, time after time.

Why do you not remember your previous lives? Well, you do not remember the early days of this life. For various reasons nature has drawn a veil of forgetfulness over our beginnings on this plane, and for excellent reasons she hides away the memory of previous lives until we are sufficiently developed to be ready to remember them. It would not be well for most people to be able to recollect their previous lives, because at the present time they simply could not stand it. Consider how prone people are to worry and grieve foolishly over the past events of this one life. Think how they fume and fret over some incident of twenty years ago when they themselves said or did something rather foolish, or when someone else illtreated them, or what not. Think how they sentimentalize and mope over "the dear dead days of long ago"; and imagine the state they would get themselves into if they had the material of many lives to handle in this way. Obviously they would destroy themselves very quickly.

The woman who cannot forget or at least forgive a mistake her husband made twenty years ago, would have a bad time with the memories of all the mistakes made by even a dozen husbands or wives in the past. The man who cannot overlook the bitter thing that his wife said ten years ago, or forgive some grievance which he holds against one of his parents, could hardly survive the accumulated remembrance of many husbands, many wives, and many parents.

And so the past is mercifully withheld from us until we reach the stage when we can regard our own histories impersonally and objectively, and when we do reach that stage it is possible to remember our previous lives. This very faculty of being able to look at our own lives in a detached way, to consider impersonally our own deeds and the things done to us by others is one of the most difficult of all things to acquire. Indeed, most people who have not studied philosophy would not even dream that such a thing could be, and yet some day you will have to attain to this, and some day you will. A time will come when you will be able to look back and consider every incident in all your lives with great interest but as calmly and unconcernedly as though they had happened to the man next door. That is the prelude to Liberation. Meanwhile, some people do get an occasional glimpse of their past incarnations in one way or another, and, if wisely handled, such glimpses can be extremely useful. And there are those who get more than a glimpse.

As a matter of fact, the whole history of all your past lives is stored away in the deeper levels of your subconscious, and thus it is that your mentality today—and consequently your destiny—is the logical outcome of all the lives that you have lived up to the present.

> Our deeds still travel with us from afar,
> And what we have been, makes us what we are.

Now we must consider the question of how the baby comes to be born in the particular family in which it is born; how you, for example, came to be born into the particular family into which you were born. Let us consider how you came to be a Jones, or a Dumont, or a Hapsburg, or whatever you are. Why, out of all the races and nations and families on the globe, were you born in just that particular family where you were born? Let me begin by saying that the stork never makes a mistake. Each one of us is born into the conditions which exactly fit his soul at the time of incarnation. He naturally gravitates to the exact spot that belongs to him.

Of course, we do not choose our parents. We go to the parents whose nature and conditions correspond with the state of the soul when it incarnates. And often that family is anything but what we would choose at that time.

It should be understood that incarnation takes place at the moment of conception. When the male principle punctures the ovum, it sets up a powerful vortex in the finer ethers, and a soul is, so to speak, sucked onto this plane and attached to the fertilized cell. Just before this the soul was waiting on the next (etheric) plane ready to incarnate. It was at the time fully conscious and it had a clear recollection of its recent life on the etheric planes, and of the main events of its last earth life. Now it is drawn onto this plane and attached to the fertilized ovum which is the nucleus of its new body. For a moment it has a preview of what the general conditions of its new life will be, and then it falls into a state of coma from which it only begins to emerge when it is born, and from which it does not completely emerge until the age of puberty.

The subconscious mind is active all the time and from the moment of incarnation it is busily building the new body, for it is the baby's own subconscious that builds its body in the uterus, and it builds it in its own image and likeness—that is why our bodies express the things that are in the soul. The mother supplies the material but the child's own soul builds its little body, and we learn in metaphysics that our environment is always but the outpicturing of our soul.

No one "sent" you to that family or selected it for you. Being the soul that you were, it was as natural and indeed as inevitable that you should go there, as it is natural for a certain drop of water on the Continental Divide to find its way ultimately into the Pacific or into the Atlantic, according to circumstances. Always remember that at the moment before birth, one is dealing, not with a new soul, but with a mature soul—the product of many lives. That soul has certain dominant characteristics, both good and bad, and under the Cosmic Law that *Like Attracts Like*, it finds its own place. Now its own place is not only the place that fits it at the time, but it is the very place that furnishes it with just the opportunity it needs to develop still further its good qualities and to overcome its weaknesses, if it so desires.

The soul gravitated to that particular family because at the beginning of its present life it had certain fundamental things in common with it. It is true that sometimes a child seems to be very much out of place in its family, but this is only an appearance. Underneath there is a fundamental family resemblance or the child would not be there. It is also true that as children grow up they usually grow apart from one another and from their parents, but, nevertheless, at the time of incarnation, there were certain fundamental similarities. Again, it is true that children are often drawn into their families by what is called a karmic link, as I shall describe later on. But this link is merely another aspect of the fact that like attracts like.

As with most of the laws of nature, the law of Reincarnation is simple in outline but extremely complicated in detail. Nevertheless, for practical purposes, a general understanding is quite sufficient. Your soul is extremely complicated. The whole of your environment and all your experiences are but the outpicturing of some of its aspects, for most of it has not come into manifestation yet. One aspect of your soul is clearly seen in your physical body, and certain underlying similarities with your parents and brothers and sisters come out in what we call family likenesses—family features and family mannerisms. Of course, we pick up many of these things by copying our elders while we are still young, but some are obviously inborn.

Now we are ready to understand the startling statement that *there is no such thing as heredity.* This statement will surprise many, but it is true. No one ever "inherits" anything from his parents or his ancestors. He already had certain mental tendencies before he incarnated this time and these tendencies guide him to a family where similar tendencies existed—that is all. The gouty subject, or the soul predisposed by its own nature to produce weak lungs, gravitates to the family having these conditions. One does not "inherit" gout or tuberculosis from his father or his grandmother; he joins a family of that type because he already has these conditions potentially. Like attracts like all through the universe, or, as we say more picturesquely, *birds of a feather flock together.*

John, with a mental quality that produces weak lungs, or gout, or a certain type of face, is taken by the stork to a family in which such mental qualities are common and which therefore outpictures these things; but that is just his opportunity to overcome the tendency to gout or tuberculosis, or to overcome or develop the particular characteristics which produce that type of face. If he does this once and for all, he will never have to meet that problem again; but he has free will and if he is foolish he will probably do nothing about it, and postpone that overcoming to a future time. It often happens, of course, that a particular child arrives in a family noted for some so-called hereditary ailment, and yet is quite free from it, though his brothers and sisters do not escape. This only means that this particular soul was not subject to that physical weakness but had other characteristics in common with that family. Jane, whose trouble is emotional instability, lands in a rather hysterical family in the same way, and this too furnishes her with just the material for understanding and overcoming her own weaknesses, if she wants to.

Thomas has certain lessons to learn which call for the struggles and difficulties that the humble people of the world have to meet, whereas William, who has already overcome these, is born into easy and comfortable circumstances—though, note carefully, he now has to learn to handle these conditions, and this may be a more difficult lesson than that of Thomas. Also William, though he is now in affluent circumstances, may someday be re-born as poor as Thomas if he does not in this life make good use of the prosperity that is his.

Social standing and human learning are of no importance in themselves except as they provide opportunities for the growth in wisdom of the soul. They come and go throughout the Long Life in accordance with the need of the day. The simple laboring man of today may well have been a prince in days gone by, a prince maybe who led a good and useful life in his own sphere but needed certain lessons that are only to be learned among the rank and file —and, incidentally, he may well be a far happier man now. The reigning prince of today may yesterday have been a poor fisherman who qualified in that character for a larger rôle upon the stage of life. We must never seek to gauge eternal values by the passing standards of time. So you yourself are your own ancestors, and at some time or other you have produced your own personal character; and all your external conditions arise out of that.

So we see how absurd it really is for people to be, as they often are, either stupidly proud or stupidly ashamed of their parents or their home. We may well be rightly proud of spiritual growth, and especially of any rapid progress that we may make, but outer conditions are in themselves of no importance. We may be wisely proud of having had worthy parents, of course, because it proves that there must have been worth in us to have deserved to have parents like that. And it is for us to see to it that we do them credit.

Reincarnation explains at once the differences in talents which we find between one man and another, just as it explains all the other differences. Why has one man a special aptitude for music, another for engineering, and yet a third for farming, while so many seem to have no particular aptitude at all? Differences in talent, like differences in opportunity, are the result of our activities in other lives. The born musician is a man who has studied music in a previous life, perhaps in several lives, and has therefore built that faculty into his soul. He is a talented musician today because he is reaping what he sowed yesterday. It may even be that in previous lives, circumstances, despite all he could do, were too strongly adverse to permit of his actually studying music; but in that case he must have had a steady, continuous *desire* to do so, and persistent desire has brought its fulfillment at last.

Child prodigies are always souls who have acquired their proficiency in a previous life; and it is noticeable how often such children are born into circumstances favorable for their talent. The child violinist often has a father with musical tastes who puts a fiddle into his hand at the earliest possible moment. The gifted child actress appears in a theatrical family, or is born right on the doorstep of Hollywood.

An understanding of Reincarnation not only solves most of life's riddles but serves as a sign-post for all sorts of questions of policy. It constantly furnishes us with guidance for the conduct of social and political life. As for one's private life, it utterly changes the perspective of the whole thing. It is the sovereign remedy for depression and discouragement and regret. It is the gospel of freedom and hope. It makes us realize that there is no mistake that cannot be repaired, that it is never too late, and that no good thing is out of reach of intelligence and work and prayer. It shows us all a future in which there is no limit to the glorious things that we may be and do. A thorough understanding of this doctrine will probably do more than anything else to improve one's character. For instance, it inevitably makes us more tolerant. We cannot but be more merciful toward other people when they displease us if we realize that very largely they are working out personal difficulties that they made in the long ago. We can realize too that no man can act "out of character," and, as misconduct or a bad disposition inevitably brings its own punishment, there is no real reason to be annoyed. When people act badly toward us, we usually think that we know better, and now we shall realize that if this is so, we must not retaliate in kind. Someone said, "When a dog bites you, you do not bite the dog to get even," and there is a great moral lesson in this. See the Presence of God in the delinquent, and forget him. Of course, this does not mean that we shall allow him to impose upon us in any way, but we shall no longer be tempted to regard him with resentment.

In general, an understanding of Reincarnation will lead us to do everything we possibly can to make the path of others easier so as to facilitate their personal evolution and that of the race. In our own lives we shall make the most of whatever talents we possess without either sighing for the impossible or fleeing from the inevitable. We shall face up to our difficulties courageously, knowing that there is no problem without a solution and that to run away is to postpone the day of reckoning.

In politics, the implications of Reincarnation are unmistakable. The best political system is the system that will give the greatest personal freedom to the individual. Each one of us must be free to work out his destiny with as little hindrance as possible from outside. Each must have every possible opportunity to exercise the qualities of initiative, self-reliance, resourcefulness, and courage. And these qualities can only be developed where the individual is free. Each must have the chance to make mistakes—and to learn from them. Each must be able to reap the fruit of his own efforts; and those who for one reason or another will not make an effort, must realize that they have to forego the fruit. No political system should put a premium upon idleness, or inefficiency, or stupidity. All the incentives should be in the direction of encouraging intelligence and industry.

The State, of course, should be conceived as existing for the benefit and protection of the individual; never should it be supposed that the individual exists for the sake of the State. On the whole, we may say that the less a government interferes in the life of the private citizen, the better will it be for all concerned. Under the compulsion of force, the individual may actually behave very correctly, because he is obliged to, but because this behavior does not arise from his own desire and initiative, it makes no permanent improvement in his character, and therefore he does not evolve.

Just as all the events of your present life are recorded in the nearer strata of the subconscious mind, so all the events of your past incarnations are recorded in much deeper strata below that. These, however, are not accessible except in very exceptional circumstances for reasons already given. Nevertheless, they are there and help to make you what you are today.

Reincarnation insures your getting all kinds of experience by playing all kinds of rôles in the great human drama. And for this reason souls usually change their nationality each time they incarnate because the different nations afford different opportunities for development. The Latin race affords certain opportunities not to be found in the Teutonic race, for example, and the Teutonic race furnishes conditions that are not to be found among Latins. In the same way, the old world of Europe presents an environment not found in the new countries, and in the New World we have opportunities (and also, of course, problems) that the people in Europe are not required to meet. We have already seen that the circumstances into which a soul is born are the natural results of his previous conduct, but this is only another way of saying that these circumstances will supply just the material he needs for further development if he will take advantage of them.

Here it may be well to issue a word of warning. There are people who make fools of themselves about Reincarnation. This is only to be expected because every great universal truth is sure to be misunderstood or misapplied by some people. A fool will wrest any piece of knowledge to his own confusion, no matter what it is. All the great truths of religion and philosophy have been caricatured by immature minds from time to time, and so we sometimes find obviously undeveloped souls claiming to be reincarnations of some of the most distinguished figures in history. I suppose we have all met the feeble-minded individual who was Shakespeare or Napoleon in his less developed days. And self-styled reincarnations of Cleopatra and Joan of Arc adorn many small tea parties up and down the country today, and bore people with their foolish talk. Of course, all this means nothing except that foolish people are finding one more opportunity to be foolish. People who really can remember previous lives are excessively reticent concerning any reference to them. Reincarnation is true and none the less so because it is sometimes misunderstood.

As you think over the truth of Reincarnation and gradually assimilate it—for an adequate realization of what this great truth really means is not to be obtained in a day or two—you will be astonished at the number of otherwise insoluble problems which it clears up. The major problems of life are logically and satisfactorily explained by Reincarnation, and all sorts of minor difficulties which have puzzled you from time to time fall easily into place too when the great scheme of things is understood.

Consider the problem of the rise and fall of nations, for example. All through history nations and empires have risen into prominence and power, have flourished for a time, and then gradually decayed. But why should this be the case? Historians have described the process, but the reasons for it have completely baffled them. The Roman Empire is an excellent example. Why did the Roman Empire "decline and fall"? Orthodox historians have not the faintest notion. They describe the fact but cannot explain it. The Goths and Vandals were able to destroy it—but why? And why not several generations sooner or later? Nobody who does not understand Reincarnation knows. Various reasons for the fall of Rome which were put forward in the past are seen today to be absurd (some people in the Middle Ages were convinced that the fall of Rome was due to the unnatural Roman habit of constantly bathing, especially in hot water!) and the experts remain baffled.

The fashion today is to make economic conditions responsible for everything, but this is to confuse cause with effect, to put the cart before the horse, because economic conditions do not produce man's mentality;

it is the human mentality that produces the economic environment. *The materialist conception of history** is one more superstition on its way to the ash-can. (The Indians lived in the same material environment that we do, but our conditions of life are entirely different from theirs because our mentalities are entirely different.) The real cause for both the rise and fall of Rome was this: For several hundred years advanced and capable souls reincarnated in the Roman nation because that group provided the best opportunity for their further development, and for the development of the race. Being the kind of people they were, they built up and organized that great world state, doing a work for humanity second to none in importance, and making great progress themselves. Then, having worked out this phase, they passed on to other activities, and an inferior grade of

*Karl Marx

souls incarnated in the Roman nation, and she gradually declined. That is the true and simple explanation.

Many of us have ourselves seen a similar process at work on a small scale. An able and energetic man spends his life building up a successful business. Then, his work done, he passes on, and he is succeeded by his son, or someone else, a person of mediocre talents or weak character, and at once the business begins to go down hill, ending finally in the bankruptcy court. One often sees the same process in connection with a social or political club or other organization. It is formed and made successful by a few capable individuals, and then for one reason or another they gradually drop out, and, being succeeded by inferior people, the enterprise gradually fails.

This, again, is the explanation of the decay of classical Greece. "The glory that was Greece" preceded "the grandeur that was Rome" into oblivion because the glorious souls who made Greece glorious went onward, and were followed by much younger and less developed souls. Of course this was really no tragedy. There would be no point racially or individually in those Greeks going on doing the same things over and over again. They passed on to learn new and different lessons, and their successors obtained an opportunity to take, what was for them, the next step. For example, Praxiteles having learned so well the lesson of artistic expression, may have reappeared hundreds of years later to learn the lessons inherent in the life of a farmer or a sailor or a merchant.

Just as like *attracts* like, so like *produces* like. This is what is called a Cosmic Law, which means that it is universally true throughout the whole of existence, not only throughout the entire physical universe, but right up through the higher planes to the Heart of God Himself. Always, like produces like. As Jesus put it, you do not gather grapes from thorns or figs from thistles; and he also said, *by their fruits ye shall know them.** So it is with our thoughts and words and deeds. As we sow, we reap. When we sow good, we reap good, and when we sow evil, we reap trouble and suffering. When we sow a little good, we reap a little good; and when we sow a great deal of good, we reap a great deal of good. When we sow a little evil, we reap a little suffering; and when we sow a great deal of evil, we reap a great deal of suffering. This is the great Law of Cause and Effect, and it is amazing that people seem to understand it as little as they do.† No one expects to sow one plant in the ground and reap another. No one expects to mix copper and tin together and get steel. No one expects to put apples and dough in the oven and get out pumpkin pie; but in the less tangible region of deeds and events, almost everyone

*Read Matthew 7: 15–20; Luke 6: 43–45.

†See card Sowing and Reaping (No. 26).

seems to think at times that he really can sow one thing and reap another. Yet the truth is that as we sow, so shall we reap, sometimes almost immediately, sometimes after a long, long interval; but always, sooner or later *like produces like.*

In the East this law of cause and effect is known as Karma and the term is a convenient one. But whatever we choose to call it, the law of nature still stands, that as we sow, we shall reap. As we have seen, the conditions into which you were born in this life are the outcome of the way in which you have lived in previous lives, and your circumstances today are the outcome of your life up to the present. It naturally follows therefore that you can be happy and well in the future if you will begin now to try to live up to the highest that you know, and take every opportunity to help and serve others in any way that may be open to you.

No matter what mistakes you have made

in the past or what opportunities you have wasted, you can overtake them all now; for your future stretches out to infinity and it is never too late with God. If you have a bad conscience about something, no matter how much evil you have sown, you can be free. Cease the wrong conduct, make whatever reparation, if any, is possible, make your peace with God, and then turn your back on the past and never think about it again. Remember that to harbor useless regrets is remorse instead of repentance, and remorse is a sin.

Note very carefully that Karma is not punishment. If you touch a red hot stove, you will burn your finger. This will hurt you, and perhaps incapacitate you for a few days, but it is not punishment, only a natural consequence. Nevertheless it is a benign and reformative thing, for after one or two such experiences in childhood, you learn to keep your fingers away from hot iron. If that stove did not hurt you, you would some day have your whole hand burned off before discovering your loss. So it is with all natural retribution—you suffer because you have a lesson to learn, but when the lesson is learned, the ill consequences cease, for nature is never vindictive.

Karma, you will now see, far from being a punishment, is really the perfect opportunity that ever-kindly nature gives us to acquire just the knowledge and experience that we need. Human beings punish one another, grown-ups punish children, and society punishes criminals; but, though we seldom suspect it, these punishments are inflicted chiefly from a desire for revenge, "to get even" with the culprit for the annoyance he has caused, even though we rationalize it in various ways. Nature never punishes; she teaches.

It is unfortunate that some people talk so much about "bad Karma." To begin with, you have seen now that no Karma is bad at all, and, further, such people are dwelling exclusively on the suffering that follows wrong conduct, and ignoring the happiness that follows upon good conduct. It is just as much the Law of Karma that every good and kind and wise thing you have ever said or done has brought you fruit of its own kind and will continue to do so. Especially every moment in your life that you have spent in prayer or meditation will continue to bless and enrich you to the end of time. Here I wish to make it as clear as I possibly can that there is nothing fatalistic about the Law of Karma. You have free will—not omnipotence, but always a choice within reasonable limits—and always you can choose the higher or the lower.

The Law of Karma teaches that by making the best use of whatever talents or advantages we have, even though they be small, we shall win still greater talents and opportunities.* On the other hand, if we

*Jesus teaches this in Matthew 25: 15–30.

neglect to make the best use of our talents and opportunities, we shall lose even what we have. The healthy man who neglects his health will lose it. The man with a musical gift who never practises his music will find some day that his gift has atrophied. The rich man who hoards up his money or spends it all selfishly on himself, instead of using it to do good to others, will either lose his money in this life or else will be born into poverty next time. God gave him that talent and he "buries it in a napkin."

Most of the trouble in our lives is not caused by Karma at all but by lack of wisdom in the present. The conditions in which you began your life were karmic, but your everyday experience is made by yourself as you go along. It is a common failing for people to behave unwisely, and then grumble at their difficulties and lay the blame on Karma. "I must have been a dreadful sinner in my last life," a person will say, "my conditions are so miserable now." And yet nine times out of ten, his miseries have nothing to do with Karma but are caused solely by poor judgment now. I knew a student of this subject who constantly talked in this way. He was the proprietor of a small business which was steadily failing, and he was surrounded by debts and other embarrassments. He was full of self-pity and he would enlarge upon his worries, and say what a terrible sinner he must have been in his last life to be "punished" in this way. Now the fact was, as some of his friends well knew, that he had no idea of running a business properly. His shop looked neglected, and the quality of his goods was inferior to that obtainable elsewhere at the same price. He was constantly out of stock of the commonest things that customers would ask for, and he was constantly borrowing money at high interest to overtake other debts. Obviously, all this had nothing to do with

Karma. His Karma, as far as it went, was good, because it had given him a business of his own in which many men would have made a great success. His trouble was poor judgment and, to some extent, laziness. Two or three of his friends who realized these facts and grew tired of his complaints, once made an effort to bring the truth home to him for his own good, but their efforts were not well received, and he could not or would not face the truth.

Success in your present life calls for good judgment, industry, and the knowledge that you are really the expression of the Living God; and no stable success can be achieved without these things.

Finally, and perhaps this is the most important point of all, you do not have to accept any set of conditions or any kind of Karma if you will rise *above* it in consciousness. Any difficulty, any dilemma, can be surmounted by whole-hearted prayer. A given difficulty can only confront you on its own level. Rise above that level through prayer and meditation and the difficulty will melt away. You do not, as so many people think, have to sit down and eat your Karma with as good grace as possible, if you can rise above that situation in consciousness. On its own level you have to accept it—you cannot transmute it *there*. But rise above any ordeal in consciousness and you will be free from it—for the Christ is Lord of Karma.*

*See *The Sermon on the Mount*, Chapter Six; and the card Scientific Prayer (No. 31).

Our birth is but a sleep and a forgetting
The Soul that rises with us, our Life's Star,
Hath had elsewhere its setting,
And cometh from afar;
Not in entire forgetfulness,
And not in utter nakedness,
But trailing clouds of glory do we come
From God, who is our home.

WORDSWORTH

The Emmet Fox Books

Emmet Fox's Golden Keys to Successful Living
Spiritual discoveries that helped millions achieve happiness; set against Emmet Fox's own life, with Reminiscences by Herman Wolhorn, friend and associate.

Power Through Constructive Thinking
27 of the above booklets and cards in one volume.

The Sermon on the Mount
This book constitutes a complete course of instruction in Scientific Christianity. This is the standard textbook. Includes the Lord's Prayer.

The Ten Commandments
Master Key to Life. A. companion volume to The Sermon on the Mount.

Find and Use Your Inner Power
Messages of help and inspiration for days of discouragement.

Make Your Life Worth While
Inspirational Messages for the Christian Life.

Alter Your Life
This book contains sixteen of the latest Emmet Fox pamphlets, plus some unpublished material.

Stake Your Claim
Short, to-the-point messages.

Around the Year with Emmet Fox
Selections from the inspiring teaching of Emmet Fox attractively arranged for daily meditation.

Diagrams For Living
Simple keys to unlocking the mysteries of the Bible and at the same time giving practical answers to the challenges of modern-day living.

The Emmet Fox Booklets

1. The Golden Key
9780875167374

2. The Seven Day Mental Diet
9780875167381

3. The Lord's Prayer
9780875167398

4. The Wonder Child
9780875167404

5. The Yoga of Love
9780875167411

6. Your Heart's Desire
9780875167428

7. The Good Shepherd
9780875167435

10. Be Still 9780875167442

11. The Secret Place
9780875167459

14. Getting Results From Prayer ~
You Must Be Born Again ~
The Great Adventures
9780875167473

18 The Magic of Tithing
9780875167480

19. The Zodiac & The Bible
9780875167497

21. How to Bring About Peace
9780875167503

24. Life After Death
9780875167510

25. Love 9780875167527

26. Sowing and Reaping
9780875167534

27. The Presence 9780875167541

28. The Word of Power
9780875167558

29. Fifteen Points 9780875167565

30. God in Business
9780875167572

31. What is Scientific Prayer?
9780875167589

33. Treatment for Divine Love
9780875167602

34. Reincarnation Described and
Explained 9780875167619

38. How to Get a Demonstration
9780875167626

44. The Seven Main Aspects of God
9780875167640

49. The Seven Days of Creation
9780875167657